Little Joe Green

A Story from *Black Beauty*,
by Anna Sewell

retold by **Stan Cullimore**
illustrated by **Tim Beer**

Chapter One

The New Stable Boy

I opened my eyes, and looked around the stable. It was morning. The sun was shining in through an open window. The air was filled with specks of dust. They came from the pile of straw that I had been lying on. I put my head down to the trough, and had a long drink of water.

From outside I could hear the sounds of the other animals waking up. I moved my tail to get rid of the flies buzzing around my head. I was just about to eat some hay when the door opened, and John Manly walked in. John is the man who looks after me. His friend, James, was with him.

"I'm getting a new stable boy," said John. "His name is Joe Green."

James laughed.

"I know Little Joe Green. He doesn't know anything about horses!"

"I know that," said John, "but I was a stable boy once. I didn't know anything about horses, either. Everyone has to learn."

James nodded, "That's true."

John picked up a brush.

"I was very lucky that the master gave me the job," he said. "Now it is my turn to give someone else a chance to learn."

"I see," said James.

John began brushing my tail.

"Little Joe Green wants a job. He says he is willing to work hard and learn, so I told him he could come and work for me."

The very next day Joe Green came into the stables. He was very young and very small. James was right. He didn't know anything about horses at all, so John had to tell him what to do all the time. But Joe worked hard and learned things quickly. He learned to sweep the stables, bring in the straw and clean the saddles.

John used to smile and say, "You learn things quickly, don't you, Joe? You will soon know as much about horses as I do!"

I was pleased to hear him say that. I liked Joe. He was a nice stable boy. He didn't know much, but he was always very kind to me and the other horses.

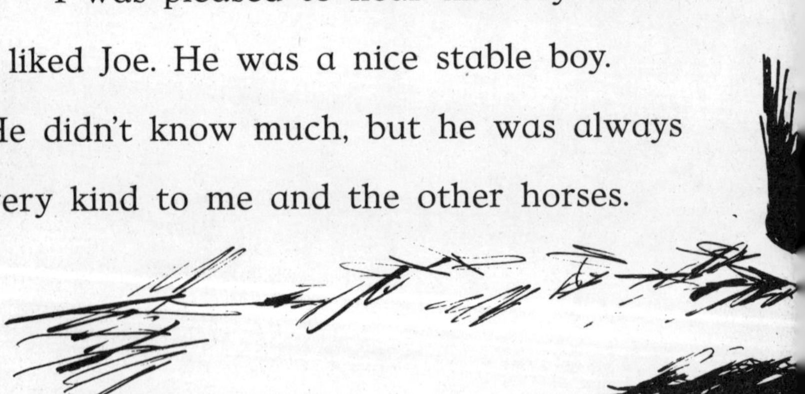

Chapter Two

Night Ride

One night I was just falling asleep when the stable door opened. John ran in. He had a letter in his hand.

"Black Beauty," he cried. "Wake up, quickly!"

I woke up right away.

"We have to take this letter to Doctor White," said John. "We must leave right away."

He threw a saddle on to my back. Then he jumped up into it.

"Beauty, I have bad news. The mistress is ill. We must get the doctor, quickly."

When I heard that the mistress was ill, I knew that I would have to go as fast as I could. Everyone loved the mistress. It would be terrible if anything happened to her.

I galloped out of the stable, and across the yard. Soon we were far away from the big house. We raced down the drive, and on to the road. The moon shone down through the trees.

The only sound to be heard was the sound of my hooves on the hard ground.

We came to the toll gate, and John shouted out, “Open the gate!”

The man came out carrying a lamp. He looked as if he had just woken up.

"Quick," shouted John. "Open the gate. We must get the doctor."

The man opened the gate, and we raced on.

We came to the long road that ran by the river.

"Now, Black Beauty, do your best," said John. I threw back my head, and went faster than I have ever gone before.

The moon shone down as I crossed the bridge into the town where the doctor lived.

We galloped down the streets, and past the houses. The church clock rang three as we got into the Market Place. We stopped by Doctor White's house. John jumped down, and rang the bell. A window shot up, and Doctor White put his head out.

"What do you want?" he asked.

"It is Mrs Gordon, sir," said John. "She is very ill. The master wants you to come at once. He thinks that she will die if you cannot get to her. Here is a note for you. He asks you to hurry."

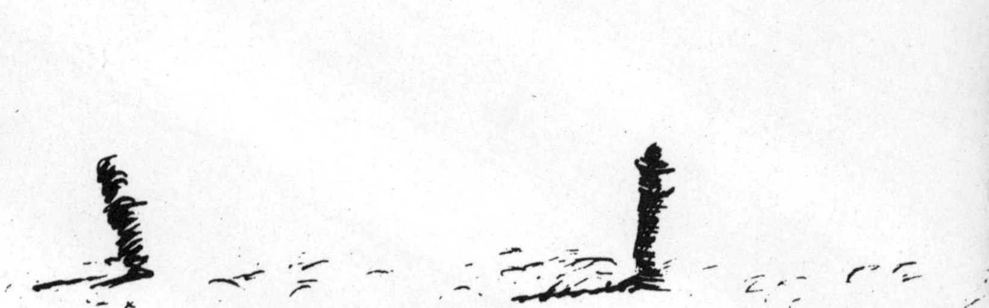

The doctor came down quickly. John gave the note to the doctor and waited. Doctor White read the note. He shook his head.

"This does not sound very good. I will get my bag."

He went back into his house. When he came back out again he had his coat on.

"I cannot use my own horse. He is not here. Can I ride Black Beauty?"

"He has raced all the way here," said John. "I would like to give him a rest, but you can ride him if there is no other horse."

"Thank you," said the doctor.

He picked up his riding whip. John took it from him.

"You won't need that, sir. Beauty knows how important this is."

I will not tell you much about the way back. The doctor was a big man, and he was not a very good rider. By the time we got to the toll gate I was very tired. The doctor stopped me.

"Have a rest, Beauty," he said.

I had a little rest, then we set off again.

When we got home to the big house, the master was waiting for us at the door. The doctor jumped down, and ran inside without saying a word. Joe Green came out, and led me back to my own stable.

Chapter Three

Black Beauty in Danger

I was very glad to be back, but I did not feel very well. My legs shook under me, and I could only stand and pant. I was sweating from head to tail. Drops ran down my legs, and I steamed all over.

"You look like a kettle on fire," said Joe.

Poor Joe! He was young and small, and he did not know very much about horses. He did the best he could, but he did not really know what to do. He rubbed my legs and back, but he did not put a nice warm cloth on me.

Then he gave me some water to drink. It was very cold, but it was very good, so I drank it all. He gave me some hay, and some corn to eat. John Manly would not have done any of those things. But Joe did not know that. He left me, and went back to bed.

Soon I began to feel worse than ever. I lay down, and began to shake all over. I felt cold and sore. How I wished for a nice warm cloth on my back. How I wished for John to come and look after me. But he was miles away, walking home.

After a long time, John came in to the stable. I gave a low moan of pain. He ran over to my side.

"Beauty, what's wrong?"

I could not tell him, but he seemed to know. He got a warm cloth, and gave me a little drink of warm water.

I heard him say to himself over and over again, "Stupid Joe! Stupid boy! He didn't put a cloth on. I bet he gave Beauty cold water to drink, too. That boy is no good. No good at all."

I was very ill, but John looked after me. He stayed by my side, and would not go away. The next day the master came to see me.

"My poor Black Beauty," he said. "My good horse. You saved Mrs Gordon's life, Beauty! Yes, you saved her."

I was glad to hear him say that. John Manly patted my back.

"Doctor White tells me that he has never seen a horse go as fast as Beauty went last night."

The master nodded.

"It is as if Beauty knew why he had to hurry," he said. Then they left, and I went to sleep.

Chapter Four

Joe's Second Chance

I do not know how for long I was ill. One day I woke up, and heard John talking with his friend, James.

"John, I wish you would say a kind word to Joe Green," said James. "He can't eat, and he can't smile. He knows it is all his fault that Beauty is ill."

John did not say a word.

"The boy did not mean to do any harm," said James. "He says that no one will ever talk to him again if Beauty dies. It goes to my heart to see him so sad."

John nodded.

“I do not want to be hard on the boy, but I can’t help it. Black Beauty is the pride of my heart. I can’t bear to see him lying so ill.”

Then he came over to me, and gave me my medicine.

“I will talk to Joe,” he said.

I did not hear anything else they said. The medicine began to do its work. I fell fast asleep. In the morning I woke up. I felt much better. John Manly came to see me.

"You look much better, Beauty," he said. "I shall go and tell Joe. He can bring you some new straw."

I soon got well again. John was very pleased. He decided to give Joe another chance. Soon Joe was sweeping the stables, bringing the straw and cleaning the saddles again. I was pleased. I always knew that one day Little Joe Green would make a very good stable boy.

Titles in *Springboard* Flyers Stage 5

Little Joe Green

Hoppers

A Place of Dark Waters

The Grinagog

Mysteries

The Making of Black Beauty

The Body Quiz

The Sharks Handbook